LOVE'S
Academy

Copyright © 2023 Sandra Jones

All Rights Reserved

Copyright © 1982 by Thomas Nelson. Used by permission. All rights reserved.; New Life Version (NLV) Copyright © 1969, 2003 by Barbour Publishing, Inc.; New Living Translation (NLT) Holy Bible, New Living Translation, copyright © 1996, 2004, 2015 by Tyndale House Foundation. Used by permission of Tyndale House Publishers, Inc., Carol Stream, Illinois 60188. All rights reserved. New King James Version®. Copyright © 1982 by Thomas Nelson. Used by permission. All rights reserved.

Acknowledgments
&
Thank You's

Thank you, Jesus, for our connection, friendship, and growth.
Thank you, Holy Spirit, for your wisdom and guidance.
I would like to give special thanks and recognition to my friend, my sister, and my goal partner, Tabresha Buggs, AKA JUSBREZZY MUSIC.

She took the videos that I made and put her skills in editing so that I can share good quality videos with the world. She is also an accountable partner when it comes to setting goals, being accountable, and even offering help when she was not working on her own projects. I told her and my BU family that I wanted to transcribe my video into words so people could read them. My Coach, Aaron Victor, told me I could turn it into a book. They all gave great ideas, but Tabresha went further and started helping me with editing since she was already doing them for her video.

Because of her support and encouragement, I was able to learn about some features that would help me turn my words into a book. I learned about Otter, signed up, and had my video transcribed into words. That became my goal on the BU call until it was done. Tabresha and I would meet regularly to talk and encourage each other to reach our goal, with no excuses or a $50 fine if not done.

She noticed lots of errors from the Otter AI and offered to edit. Because she had her own dreams and goals, I finally went to Fiverr for editing and Press N' Sow for help with my Devotional. Tabresha was a big part of me completing my book, and we both got even more inspired to write our own stories in the future. Thank you, my sister, for our mutual friendship and the support that we have for each other. Two is better than one because when one falls down, the other can lift them up. Thank you, Jesus for our connection, friendship, and growth. Thank you, Holy Spirit, for wisdom and guidance

Welcome & Share

welcome

welcome to the devotional & journal

share

share the journal with someone that you know!

get ready!

get ready to shift from your current position
to "the place" where you will grow!

DECLARATION OF TRANSFORMATION

I declare that I will allow God to transform me from the inside out. As I dedicate spending time with Him daily, I will use the power of His word to become a new creation. I will surrender all of my fears, worries, and anxieties to Him, knowing He is faithful and true and can provide me with everything I need.

I recognize that transformation begins with a choice, a decision to move forward in faith. So I declare that I will no longer be held back by my old ways but instead choose to live a life of freedom and purpose in the love of God. I know that transformation is an ongoing process, so I commit to seeking wisdom through His word, prayer, and devotion today.

I declare that I will be a conduit for God's love in the world, radiating His light and leading others toward true transformation. With courage, faith, strength, and grace, I will be an example of what it looks like to have hope in Jesus Christ.

Thank you, Lord, for transforming how I think, speak, believe, and live. Amen.

Psalm 139:13-14
English Standard Version
13 For you formed my inward parts;
you knitted me together in my
mother's womb.
14 I praise you, for I am fearfully
and wonderfully made.
Wonderful are your works;
my soul knows it very well.

INTRODUCTION

I am Sandra Jones and:

I am fearfully and wonderfully made!
I am the head and not the tail.
I am above and not beneath.
I can do ALL things through Christ who strengthens me.
I understand everything that my eyes see- I see Kingdom visions.
I envision everything that my ears hear-
I hear the call of GOD on my life, and I obey
I understand everything that my hands touch —
I write the vision, and GOD will bring it to pass.
I am consistent. I am a lover of humankind.
I am healthy, I am wealthy, and I am wise.

I am the founder and spokesperson for Love's Academy-an organization created to uplift and empower through encouragement and support. Encouraging Word of the Day is a series of 30-day daily devotionals that will inspire you to develop into more of who you were born to be. Our heart desires to share the love that we have for people in a way that is practical, personal, and understandable.

In this devotional, we want to invigorate you to live life and enjoy each day it brings. Words from time in prayer and meditation inspire this book. We know that life has more to offer than what we can see with our eyes and more than what we may experience through our feelings.

In the past, I felt like my life had no meaning. I felt like I was wasting a lot of time doing nothing. Because I wanted to make a change and a real impact, I started making daily devotional videos that I had edited by a friend and began to post daily on Facebook.

The positive energy and growth we saw in ourselves due to the videos, we knew we needed to make what helped us available to others. We had begun transforming our lives and wanted the same for others! I didn't let the fact that I had never published a book stop me. What was important was to get messages of hope and inspiration out there. Writing is an example of what can happen when you pursue a goal.

We want to motivate you to get up and get going daily. All you need is a little time and commitment to yourself. It's time to de-clutter the thoughts of your mind and start writing down what's in your heart. When you write your thoughts and ideas, you can begin planting the seeds that will grow as time goes on. Then, you have to do the work to bring them to life.

Each day's encouraging word starts with a relevant scripture from the Holy Bible and ends with a question that will hopefully spark a new and exciting turnaround for you. Sometimes all it takes is a flicker to ignite the most incredible ideas of change. At Love's Academy, we challenge you today to envision yourself expanding into more of who you are to be. We pray that you continue to feel more entitled each day to go after your heart's desires!

Praying for You,
Sandra Jones

The How

Here is how to use this devotional.

Bible Scriptures used in this devotional came from several different versions of the Holy Bible as follows: (KJV) King James Version, (NLV) New Living Translation, and (NIV) New International Version. To get the most out of this book, we encourage you to be intentional about spending quality time by taking time to yourself for this devotional. Next, get a designated time and space that you can go to daily for the next 30 days to be alone and comfortable.

This devotional includes the QR code for you to see and hear this powerful devotional. Right here and right now is Holy time for you and the Lord. These videos are designed to use your sight, hearing, and speaking senses. With your mouth, you will speak and praise GOD for what HE has already done and what He will do for you. Being thankful and giving praise to GOD is what will give you that encouragement to encourage others.

Remember to use this time and space to create a habit-stacking effect. To measure where you started, keep a journal to track your thoughts, ideas, dreams, and progress. There will be growth that is noticeable and worth capturing. You may be inspired to write a book about your growth journey.

We have provided a small amount of space for you to jot down notes here, but take 20 minutes of quiet and private time so that you can focus on yourself. Write down how you feel and one thing you can do to help someone else.

LOVE'S ACADEMY
DAILY VIDEOS

SCAN ME

DAY 1

Do The Work

The encouraging word for you today is Do the Work. Do the work it will take to get the job done. Have you ever said to yourself that you're going to achieve a sure thing one day, but you have yet to get around to doing any of the things that would accomplish it?

For instance, if you're saving for a house, you must work and make money. You know that you have present bills that you have to pay and want to save for the home you want to get. That takes a solid plan. Start by asking friends or loved ones who have done what you aspire to do about what steps they took. Write down what you learned, then formulate your action plan. Once you have done that, commit to doing whatever other measures are required to get it done.

I encourage you to do the work it takes to have the right to have what you want. It's totally up to you.

James 2:26
For as the body without the spirit is dead, so faith without works is dead also.

Journal

How will you demonstrate your faith?

_____

_____

_____

_____

_____

_____

_____

_____

_____

_____

_____

_____

_____

_____

My Prayer Today

Date: _____

DAY 2

Don't Let Your Past Failures...

The encouraging word for you today is Don't Let Your Past Failures Keep You From Taking Your Next Step. We often don't take that next step because we think about past failures. What we can do instead is be future-focused.

What next step could you take to contribute to your future reality? If you're fearful, pray for the courage to take your next step. It's ok to have past failures but move on from them. That's why they're called the past. You can't do anything about that. But what you can do is learn from it and move forward. Learn to forgive yourself and remember you will always have wins and losses.

When things don't go how we'd like, we usually get an opportunity to learn an important lesson. So I am here to encourage you today, do not, I repeat, do not let your past failures defeat you- Let them improve you.

1 John 4:4
You are from God, little children, and have overcome them, because greater is He who is in you than he who is in the world.

Journal

Considering something you recently overcame,
what next step will you take in that journey?

_____

_____

_____

_____

_____

_____

_____

_____

_____

_____

_____

_____

_____

_____

My Prayer Today

Date: _____

DAY 3

Forgive as God Forgave You

The encouraging word for you today is Forgive as GOD Forgave You. So often, we want to hold on to grudges or get mad at what people do to us. We can hold feelings of resentment or anger towards others. Sometimes relationships are lost for a lifetime because of a lack of willingness on our part, or another's, to forgive. What about what we have done to GOD?

I have often fallen short of what He has asked of me, yet He is always faithful, willing, and ready to forgive me. God loves me. GOD has forgiven me so many times. I have to learn how to forgive just like GOD forgave me. I am the image of GOD; therefore, I have to act like Him. I have to think like Him, and I have to forgive like Him.

So the encouraging word I have for you today is to learn to forgive as GOD forgave you. Don't hold grudges, or grudges will keep you- in captivity.

Colossians 3:13
Bear with each other and forgive one another if any of you has a grievance against someone. Forgive as the Lord forgave you.

Journal

Who in your life could be healed today by your forgiveness?

_____

_____

_____

_____

_____

_____

_____

_____

_____

_____

_____

_____

_____

_____

_____

_____

_____

_____

_____

_____

My Prayer Today

Date: _____

DAY 4

Planting Seeds

The encouraging word for you today is Planting Seeds. You may think, "Is it time to plant seeds?" Yes. It's always time to plant seeds of love and empowerment. It's always time to plant seeds of inspiration. When you talk to someone and tell them something positive, you put thought into their head. You're planting the seed.

So, you can produce a source of encouragement, a seed of enlightenment, or a seed of imagination. But whatever you do, ensure you're planting the good seed, watering it, and feeding it. Check on it, then water it again. After encouraging someone about something they seem incredibly excited about, go back and check on them later to see how they're doing with that word or that seed. It may need a little sprinkle from you to sprout!

Sometimes knowing someone cares and supports what they are trying to do is enough to keep them going. Be the friend or loved one you'd want to have.

Ecclesiastes 11:6
In the morning sow your seed, and at evening withhold not your hand; for you do not know which will prosper, either this or that, or whether both alike will be good.

Journal

What good seeds are you sowing?

_____

_____

_____

_____

_____

_____

_____

_____

_____

_____

_____

_____

My Prayer Today

Date: _____

DAY 5

Power to Discover You

The encouraging word for you today is Power to Discover You. You have the power to speak, think, and make decisions. You also have the power to discover who you are to become. What are the critical choices that you have made about how you will live your life? Have you changed your mind about something important to you because of something said to you? Remember your core values. What do you believe? Refrain from being persuaded by what someone else is doing, thinking, or saying.

GOD has given us the freedom to choose for ourselves. Choose the life that you want. You have that GOD-given power within you. Use the power in your words, thoughts, and actions.

If you aren't feeling hopeful, choose to have a renewed mindset. You are not the same person you were an hour ago. You have a new way of thinking.

2 Corinthians 5:17
Therefore if any man be in Christ, he is a new creature: old things have passed away; behold, all things have become new.

Journal

What will you ask GOD today to reveal to you about yourself when you pray?

_____

_____

_____

_____

_____

_____

_____

_____

_____

_____

_____

_____

_____

_____

My Prayer Today

Date: _____

DAY 6

What's in Your Heart?

The encouraging word for you today is, What's in Your Heart? Did you know that out of the abundance of the heart, your mouth will speak? When you say positive and enlightening thoughts, you will see manifestations of those thoughts. My heart is so full of ideas that will benefit me and others. I'm so grateful to GOD that out of the abundance of my heart, my mouth began to speak.

I began to say those good things and framed what I wanted to see in the future. I began to see a picture forming in my imagination. As a result of that, we now have Love's Academy. You can shape your thoughts and become or do whatever you want to. What's your desired outcome? Be sure you are speaking about those things that will bring life.

Remain positive and hopeful, regardless of what things may seem like at the time. Search your heart to begin speaking those words of life for yourself.

Luke 6:45
A good person produces good out of the good stored up in his heart. An evil person produces evil out of the evil stored up in his heart, for his mouth speaks from the overflow of the heart.

Journal

What can you speak from the abundance of your heart?

My Prayer Today

Date: _____

DAY 7

Stay in the Light

Great morning, family and friends.

The word that I have for you today is Stay in The Light. Light will always dispel darkness. Light will always win out over darkness. I promise you; things may be a little dark now, but they will get lighter. You have to believe that they will get better. You're looking at other people saying that they got this, and they got that. What are they going through? What did they do to get that?

Some of that stuff, I promise you, you do not want. It looks like the glamor of fame, but it can be all fake. Don't believe the hype. Stay in the light. You can do it. Just keep on, stand on your word, believe in God's promises, and stay around people who will be positive and will tell you what you should not do. You already know you shouldn't be doing them, so don't get around people who will encourage you to do the wrong things. Stay in the light. You got this.

I am Sandra Jones, and I am here to encourage you today. Girl, you better stay in this light. Stay in the light.

Galatians 5:26
Let us not become conceited, provoking and envying each other.

Journal

What steps can you take to ward off envy in your life?

_____

_____

_____

_____

_____

_____

_____

_____

_____

_____

_____

_____

_____

My Prayer Today

Date: _____

DAY 8

How much do you do?

The encouraging word for you today is how much do you do? So many times, we say we are too busy to help people experiencing poverty or feed those who may be hungry. Too busy to volunteer at church or keep our sister's kids, though we do it to help out. The real question is, how much love do we put into what we're doing?

Helping people is something other than something you do to check something off your list. People can tell the difference when you're helping because you care versus helping to be seen. My encouraging word for you today is to put some love into it when you're helping. Sometimes when we are helping others, they may not be able to express gratitude, complaining the whole time that we're helping them. To you, it may be frustrating. In these times, thank GOD for all he has done for you.

Remembering helps foster a better attitude so that you are not irritated when helping someone who is not being so kind in return. We are here to help one another.

Hebrews 13:16
And do not forget to do good and to share with others for with such sacrifices God is pleased.

Journal

Who do you know that would be blessed by your help today?

My Prayer Today

Date: _____

DAY 9

Power in Praise

The encouraging word for you today is Power in Praise. Sometimes we don't want to get up in the morning because we're still tired. We may think, "This is not going to be a good day." Changing your mindset, praising GOD, and being thankful you could open your eyes can turn your day around. I start saying, "GOD, thank you for waking me up. Thank you for giving me the strength to get out of this warm, cozy bed that I have." Then I started to think of other things to be thankful for and would praise GOD for that. "Thank you for the grace you've given me throughout my life. Thank you for protecting my family and me from hurt, harm, and danger." I end my day the same way.

There is power in praising GOD, thanking Him, and worshiping Him. I am grateful that He allowed me to start a business and gave me the ability to learn things and apply them. Start praising your way through everything--hurt, negativity, and loneliness.

Psalm 100:4
Enter into HIS gates with thanksgiving and into HIS courts with praise, give thanks to HIM and praise HIS name.

Journal

What will you break through today by praising GOD?

_____

_____

_____

_____

_____

_____

_____

_____

_____

_____

_____

_____

_____

_____

My Prayer Today

Date: _____

DAY 10

Divine Imagination

The encouraging word for you today is Divine Ideas. The Bible talks about having an imagination. In my accountability group, we talk about wild thoughts. Anything that I put in my mind to imagine, I can have it. What is a fantastic idea for you? Have you ever thought about precisely what you wanted to do in life without setting limits on it? Can you see it? Whatever you imagine in your heart and mind, you can create. It will take work and persistence through obstacles. It is good to have the support of friends and loved ones, but be careful how you share your dreams.

Sometimes you can't tell people what you imagine because they may say things to discourage you. I'm here to challenge you. Think higher than what you can see. Have a divine imagination. Think of the one place where you would like to go and what you want to do. Start imagining that regularly. Once you can see it, plan to do it. Because you got that imagination working for you, it will come to fruition.

Start imagining it right now!

Colossians 3:2
Set your mind on things that are above, not on things that are on earth.

Journal

What can you imagine that GOD has for you?

_____

_____

_____

_____

_____

_____

_____

_____

_____

_____

_____

_____

_____

My Prayer Today

Date: _____

DAY 11

Follow the Leader

The encouraging word for you today is, Be Careful Who You Follow. When you follow a leader, you must ensure that that leader has good direction, a map, and a plan. You can only follow some people. That leader may sound and look good, but you will find out once you get on that road. Please stay within reach, as turning back may seem impossible. So be careful who you follow. Ensure your leaders have the credentials to lead in the area you want to follow. Can they conduct themselves?

Once, while teaching in Sunday School, when we went to play 'Follow the Leader,' a student asked to be the leader. His little brother recalled a time they lost a battle in a video game when his brother was the leader who led them to their death. He said he had learned his lesson and would not follow him anymore. That can happen in life. **Follow the GODLY behavior that you see.**

Matthew 20:26
It shall not be this way among you. But whoever wishes to become a great leader, must become a servant.

Journal

Who or what are you following that may lead you wrong?

_____

_____

_____

_____

_____

_____

_____

_____

_____

_____

_____

_____

_____

My Prayer Today

Date: _____

DAY 12

Have Confidence in Yourself

The encouraging word for you today is to Have Confidence in Yourself. You may say, "Sandra, how can I have self-confidence when I don't feel confident?" Well, start by being the best version of yourself. Do whatever it takes to feel your best. Don't be worried about what other people think about you. If your hair's too short or too long, if you're big or if you're small, the way you wear your clothes or the way you wear your hairstyle. Be confident in being yourself.

We may often compare ourselves to others and feel a lack of confidence because we need more skill in a particular area. Build your confidence by reading God's word and learning who He says you are. Short or tall, big or small, don't worry about what other people are or what they aren't saying about you.

Psalms 27:3
Though a host encamps against me, my heart shall not fear; though war arises against me, I will be confident.

Journal

In what areas will you ask God to strengthen your confidence?

_____

_____

_____

_____

_____

_____

_____

_____

_____

_____

_____

_____

My Prayer Today

Date: _____

DAY 13

The Needs of Others

The encouraging word for you today is The Needs of Others. Do you know anyone that has any need? You may have needs, but did you know that if you place the needs of others before your own, you are making a sacrifice? Our parents sacrificed so much for us. They even went without things so we could have what we needed.

Jesus did the same thing for us. He gave up himself just for us to meet the need to bring us back to GOD. So my encouraging word for you today is to do what you can to help supply the needs of others. Help them out. Show them that there is someone who cares for them.

One day, someone else is going to place your needs first. Try it and see what happens for you. Remember someone else today. Sometimes we think we're bad off until we remember someone suffering worse than us. Some people don't have a family or anyone to look after them.

Matthew 7:12
Jesus says, "so in everything, do to others what you would have them do to you, for this sums up the Law and the Prophets."

Journal

What can you do today to help fill someone's need in place of your wants?

_____

_____

_____

_____

_____

_____

_____

_____

_____

_____

_____

_____

_____

My Prayer Today

Date: _____

DAY 14

Hazard

The encouraging word for you today is Hazard. What happens when your building needs to be corrected? It may fall and hurt someone. What is a hazard in your life? Is it a friendship you know has reached its end but don't know how to do it?

Sometimes you feel like you're taking risks when you have uncomfortable conversations with your children. How would they respond, or how could it get out of hand? We take insurance out on our vehicles and homes. We should ensure our relationships with people and GOD. Studying the Bible teaches us how to have a relationship with GOD and man.

If you have identified a hazard, figure out how it got there, then work to overcome it. Figuring out the problem will help to avoid repeating it. Decide what you need to do. If you need help finding a solution, ask for help.

Mark 8:36
For what does it profit a man to gain the whole world and forfeit his soul.

Journal

What is in life that you thought was a gain but now realize is a hazard?

_____

_____

_____

_____

_____

_____

_____

_____

_____

_____

_____

_____

_____

_____

My Prayer Today

Date: _____

DAY 15

A Refreshing Surprise

The encouraging word for you today is, A Refreshing Surprise. Has someone ever done something for you or said something to you that just gave you the refreshment you needed? You may have been down and out. You may have been ready to give up and would throw it all away. But then you heard a word that was so refreshing that it turned you entirely around. It could be something you may have seen, heard, or experienced.

I'm here to tell you today that GOD sends people to refresh us. It is a refreshing surprise when someone tells you something great, giving you that hope and that light. A little light could allow you to see the end of the tunnel. Have you ever taken advantage of an opportunity to be a refreshing surprise to someone?

When GOD uses people to be a blessing, we need to remember to be a blessing to others. Think of how good you feel when you make someone else smile.

Do it today!

1 Corinthians 12:31
But desire the greater gifts. And I will show you an even better way.

Journal

What surprising gift has GOD revealed to you?

My Prayer Today

Date: _____

DAY 16

Limits

The encouraging word for you today is Limits. We have a speed limit; you can't go past it without risking consequences. The law sets the speed limit. What limits have you set for yourself? Make sure you limit the time to give to others and keep some of that time for yourself.

Limit the stress you expose yourself to while parenting, working your job, or talking to people who may have problems. What are your limits? Set those limits today and make sure that no one goes past them. When going after your goals, remember that GOD is your source, and He will help you obtain everything you need and want to attain in life. Set those limits high above the clouds.

Anything that you set your mind to do, you can accomplish. You can be limitless by putting limits on everyone else. Remove the limits that you have set in your mind on what you can do. Remember, you can do all things through Christ Jesus, who strengthens you!

Matthew 19:26
But Jesus looked at them and said, "with man this is impossible, but with God all things are possible.

Journal

What limits will you re-evaluate today?

_____

_____

_____

_____

_____

_____

_____

_____

_____

_____

_____

_____

My Prayer Today

Date: _____

DAY 17

You Are Not a Puppet

The encouraging word for you today is, You Are Not a Puppet. Be careful when people give you gifts, as strings may be attached. You can tell when a string is attached because they want something in return. If you see what seems to be a string, ask, "What is this? Is there something attached to this?"

Make sure you understand the intention behind the gift. You don't have to take advantage of every gift, and it's ok to refuse one that doesn't feel right. When you give, are you genuine? When GOD gives you an idea and a plan, I promise He will provide for that plan if you do it his way.

Have discernment regarding people wanting to be part of your life or business. Listen to the Holy Spirit today, don't delay. You are not a puppet, nor are you to be played or manipulated. If you find yourself tugged, remove the strings.

Titus 3:10
Reject a factious man after a first and second warning.

Journal

Who has fed your spirit that you should be spending
more time around?

_____

_____

_____

_____

_____

_____

_____

_____

_____

_____

_____

_____

_____

_____

My Prayer Today

Date: _____

DAY 18

Thanks, but no thanks

Matthew 5:37 Let what you say be simple, 'yes or no'? Anything more than this comes from evil.

Great morning, family and friends. The word I have for you today is, Thanks but No Thanks. People often give you something, and you say, "Aw, thank you. That was so kind of you." And then you get further down the road and say, "Hey, what's going on here?" Sometimes it's good to say, "No, thank you." Listen, please don't take advantage of people. If you know that they're giving you something because they care for you, like you, or are trying to build a relationship with you, stop taking those gifts.

Girls, come on now. You know that you shouldn't have accepted it in the first place. My word for you today is to say thanks but no thanks. Sometimes it comes at a cost, and it's not worth hurting someone's feelings, especially when they're giving because they care about you and they want to build a relationship with you.

It's not always to get something in return, but they're just trying to show you their compassion and trying to show you how much they care for you. Stop taking those gifts people give you; you know you don't like them. Stop doing that. Just say thank you, but no thanks.

I am Sandra Jones, and I am fearfully and wonderfully made.

Proverbs 11:14
Where no counsel is, the people fall: but there is safety in the multitude of counsellors.

Journal

How can you start asking for help today?

_____

_____

_____

_____

_____

_____

_____

_____

_____

_____

_____

_____

My Prayer Today

Date: _____

DAY 19

Victory

The encouraging word for you today is victory. "V-i-c-t-o-r-y, victory, victory, victory!" Remember that victory song from when you were in school? Have you ever had a morning filled with victories? You woke up on time; you got on your video call on time. You answered your emails; you got some great responses from emails you sent out earlier that week. It's just been a victory day.

My encouraging word for you is to stay in that victory. Consider what you did to win that day, and then repeat those things. Decide to remain positive. It starts with having a restful night. And a victorious day. Pursue the next victory in your life. You got this.

When you have a victory, please write it down so you can have a log to remember what you have won. Writing it helps keep your momentum going and keeps you grateful.

Remember, you did it once, and you can do it again.

1 Corinthians 15:57
But thanks be to GOD! He gives us the victory through our LORD JESUS CHRIST.

Journal

What action step can you take today that will lead to your next victory?

_____

_____

_____

_____

_____

_____

_____

_____

_____

_____

_____

_____

_____

My Prayer Today

Date: _____

DAY 20

Reset

The encouraging word for you today is Reset. Is it time to reset?

Did you ever start on a journey and, halfway through, figure out that it's not really what you wanted? I encourage you today to stop wasting time. Stop what you're doing and think. Make sure that it's something that you know you want to do. You should see signs of progress or evidence that you are going the right way. If none exist, save yourself time and possibly more money. Just go ahead and count that as a learning lesson and move forward. It's not a loss because you learned one thing you don't want to do.

Remember that every loss doesn't have to end as a loss. Let it be a learning experience. Next time, plan, research, and get the information on what you want, not just for the money it could bring. If you chase money, you'll never catch it.

Don't chase the money; Chase the process.

Isaiah 43:18-19

Remember not the former things, nor consider the things of old. Behold, I am doing a new thing; now it springs forth, do you not perceive it? I will make a way in the wilderness and rivers in the desert.

Journal

What part of your life could use a reset today?

_____

_____

_____

_____

_____

_____

_____

_____

_____

_____

_____

_____

_____

My Prayer Today

Date: _____

DAY 21

You Are Comforted

The encouraging word for you today is, You Are Comforted. Have you ever had someone to comfort you, hold you, or say some words that just gave you comfort in your spirit? That's what we should strive for, not only to receive comfort but to give comfort to others. It's important to have a support system filled with love and comfort.

There are so many things we face daily that, emotionally and mentally, it can take a toll. But it's so amazing when you can think about the goodness of GOD and how He comforts you, reassures you, and gives you promises in His word. And then, once you find those promises in His words, speak those words out loud. Meditate on it day and night, and you begin to believe it as you see it.

Thank GOD for making good on what He said He would do for you. Thank Him for the healing that His love has provided. You will feel comfortable in your spirit. Take the time to comfort someone and see how it will comfort you.

Isaiah 26:3
Thou wilt keep him in perfect peace, whose mind is stayed on thee: because he trusteth in thee.

Journal

In what way can you be comforting today?

_____

_____

_____

_____

_____

_____

_____

_____

_____

_____

_____

_____

My Prayer Today

Date: _____

DAY 22

Follow Your Plan

The encouraging word for you today is to Follow Your Plan. Yes, I said follow your plan. Please sit down, think about the things you want to take place and plan it out. You may have a coach or someone to work with you on your plan. Maybe you are trying to go at it alone. Don't do that. Everyone needs help sometimes. Be sure to write it in detail, then ask someone to read it to ensure your plan is clear.

When you get on that path following your plan, stay with it. Stick to what you've studied and what you've learned works. Remember the things you've received excellent advice. And then be careful when other people come in and start giving you more advice. It may not be time for that advice. You have to be careful to follow the plan. Don't change so quickly with every piece of knowledge or information you get. It's called a plan for a reason.

Work on your plan. With GOD's help, that's the plan that will work. I promise you if you have a plan that GOD gave you, and you write it down and don't stop, it will happen in due time. Pray about your decisions and listen to what GOD has to say.

Psalm 33:11
The plans of the LORD stand firm forever, the purposes of His heart through all generations.

Journal

Do your plans line up with GOD'S plan?

_____

_____

_____

_____

_____

_____

_____

_____

_____

_____

_____

_____

_____

My Prayer Today

Date: _____

DAY 23

Inseparable

The encouraging word for you today is Inseparable.

Do you know that nothing can separate us from the love of GOD? There are a lot of things that we separate from, but GOD is not one of them. We may separate from a spouse, kids, or even a job. It is an expected part of life to win sometimes and lose sometimes.

Sometimes we feel abandoned by friends or family members. GOD is always available to fill those empty spaces in our lives. Not even death itself can separate us from the love of GOD. So, I encourage you to develop that relationship today and get to know GOD. Get to know His goodness. Get to know all the benefits of being in love. The love GOD has for us, no man or situation can break.

Get into your word and find out who GOD is to you so that you can have that inseparable relationship. That's the only relationship that can truly never be severed.

Romans 8:38
And I am convinced that nothing can ever separate us from God's love. Neither death nor life, neither angels nor demons, neither our fears for today nor our worries about tomorrow-not even the powers of hell can separate us from GOD'S love.

Journal

What steps can you take today to move closer to God?

_____

_____

_____

_____

_____

_____

_____

_____

_____

_____

_____

_____

My Prayer Today

Date: _____

DAY 24

It's Not Over

The encouraging word for you today is, It's Not Over. It's not over until life is over. As long as you have breath in your body, you can do what you want. It's not over for you. If you need to clean up your house, you have time to do that. It's not over.

Suppose you want to take a week-long trip to Hawaii; you can because it's not over. You may be thinking, "Have you looked at the news lately with all this stuff going on? It is over." I'm here to tell you that regardless of what you see on the news, it's not over. You can't live in fear. Based on what you see online, it may be true, or it may be false. I am not suggesting you fail to take precautions because you must. While you should always consider safety, you have got to continue living. You have to live your life knowing without a doubt that life is worth fighting for until its end. You have what you think, and you have what you say.

So, I'm encouraging you today to live life to the fullest. Live life like it's just getting started.

Proverbs 3:5
Trust in the LORD with all your heart and lean not on your own understanding.

Journal

What dreams will happen today if you truly believe it's not over?

_____

_____

_____

_____

_____

_____

_____

_____

_____

_____

_____

_____

_____

_____

My Prayer Today

Date: _____

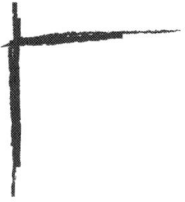

DAY 25

Joy

The encouraging word for you today is Joy. When we talk about joy, what comes to mind for you? Do you have joy when everything is going your way? Is it joy that you experience when people are giving you things? Real joy comes from the inside. You may not always be happy about your situation, but you can still have joy. Joy is not something that comes from the world. Therefore, the world can't take it away.

When I think of GOD'sgoodness, I can't help but feel gratitude. As I continue to recall those times and thank Him repeatedly, I feel the joy of healing.   I experience the joy of growth and change. As I grow older, I share the joy of aging. There are things to be joyous about all around us all the time. Life can be good or bad, but you don't have to let the circumstances rob you of your joy.

Change your perspective and watch it change your mood. Start thinking back and getting joyful. My word for you today is don't just be happy– have some joy.

Nehemiah 8:10
The Joy of the LORD is your strength.

Journal

What blessing do you want to praise God for today?

_____

_____

_____

_____

_____

_____

_____

_____

_____

_____

_____

_____

My Prayer Today

Date: _____

DAY 26

Just One Thing

The encouraging word for you today is Just One Thing. Just set one goal today. Create your plan, work at it, and your goal is attainable. There are so many things that we need to get done. We may start with five or six things until they are complete. If we name one thing that we're going to do and do that thing until completion, we can mark that goal as accomplished and cross it off our list.

Today my goal was to clean out my office, but on the way to the office, I saw some dishes in the sink, so I stopped and started to wash those. I noticed some books on the kitchen table and returned them to my room. Then I said that I needed to straighten out my bookshelf. One thing turned into many things. If I had stayed focused on just one thing, I would have cleaned the home office by now.

Just do one thing.

Psalm 27:4
One thing I have desired of the LORD, that will I seek after; that I may dwell in the house of the LORD all the days of my life.

Journal

What one thing will you do today?

My Prayer Today

Date: _____

DAY 27

Knowing Is Not Enough

The encouraging word for you today is Knowing Is Not Enough. Just because you know how something works doesn't mean it's enough to get you through. You may know how to make your bed, but you need to apply that knowledge to make your bed.

You may know you're supposed to love your neighbor, but you must help meet their needs when you have the means to do it. You may know you're supposed to get to work on time, but you'll be late if you wait to set your alarm clock the night before and get proper rest. Knowing is only half the battle; application is the rest. Let's not waste what we know.

I encourage you today to take what you know, apply that knowledge and see how it makes a difference not only in your own life but in the life of others.

Proverb 2:6
For the LORD gives wisdom; from his mouth comes knowledge and understanding;

Journal

What knowledge can you apply today?

My Prayer Today

Date: _____

DAY 28

Let's Talk

The encouraging word for you today is Let's Talk. When was the last time you had a girls' day or night, and you just talked about what was going on with your life? Maybe it was two of you; maybe it was three of you. When was the last time that you poured out your heart to someone so that you could figure out what was going on with your life?

Do you also offer a listening ear and allow them to vent and figure out what's happening with that person's life? Talk to someone so you don't have it all bundled up. And for the guys, have a guys' day or night out. Take time to talk to your guy friends and tell them what's going on. The more we speak with those we can trust, the more we learn about each other and how to help each other better. Because sometimes two minds are better than one.

My word for you today is let's talk. Let's genuinely have a good talk.

Ecclesiastes 4:9-10
Two are better than one, because they have a good reward for their labor. For if they fall, the one will lift up his fellow.

Journal

Who are the people in your life who could mutually benefit from your listening ear?

_____

_____

_____

_____

_____

_____

_____

_____

_____

_____

_____

_____

_____

My Prayer Today

Date: _____

DAY 29

Mindful

The encouraging word for you today is Mindful. What does it mean to you when someone is mindful of you? I found out this morning that I am always on somebody's mind. He's always thinking about me. He always has my best interests at heart, no matter the situation. He knows what I am doing, feeling, thinking, where I am going, and how He can help me. That person is Jesus Christ.

I found out that I'm always on his mind. Isn't it good to know that you're always on GOD's mind, whether everything is going well and if things seem like they are going wrong? You are always a priority on GOD's mind. You should realize that you are so unique that someone always has you on their mind. His mind and that someone is GOD. That someone is Jesus Christ, our Lord, and Savior.

So the next time you think that no one ever thinks about you, remember there is someone who never stops thinking about YOU. Be mindful of that fact.

Philippians 2:5-11
Let this mind be in you, which was also in Christ Jesus:

Journal

Knowing you're always on GOD's mind, what fears will you put away?

_____

_____

_____

_____

_____

_____

_____

_____

_____

_____

_____

_____

_____

My Prayer Today

Date: _____

DAY 30

Give While You Live

The encouraging word for you today is Give While You Live. How often have we said we will do something and don't take the time to do it? Maybe we say that we're going to take care of a person and take them shopping, buy them some clothes, or spend some time and they pass away before we do it. Then we think, "Man, I wished I would have given while they were still alive."

I'm encouraging you today to give while you live. Give your time by volunteering at the women's or a local homeless shelter. Take advantage of the opportunities to give to others while you live. Give to people who can use your support. Take the time to make a phone call. Please take your time with the other person or yourself. I promise that when you take time to give to others, it will make you both feel better.

Continue the cycle of life. Just give while you live.

Acts 20:35
In all things I have shown you that by working hard in this way we must help the weak and remember the words of the Lord Jesus, how HE himself said, "it is more blessed to give than to receive."

Journal

Who can you give to today?

_____

_____

_____

_____

_____

_____

_____

_____

_____

_____

_____

_____

My Prayer Today

Date: _____

Made in the USA
Columbia, SC
13 August 2023

21512709R00072